ISO/IEC 38500
The IT governance standard

ISO/IEC 38500
The IT governance standard

ALAN CALDER

IT Governance Publishing
IT Governance Limited
Unit 3, Clive Court
Bartholomew's Walk
Cambridgeshire Business Park
Ely
Cambridgeshire
CB7 4EH
United Kingdom

www.itgovernance.co.uk

First published in the United Kingdom in 2008
by IT Governance Publishing

ISBN 978-1-905356-57-7

ABOUT THE AUTHOR

Alan Calder is a leading author on IT governance and information security issues. He is chief executive of IT Governance Limited, the one-stop shop for books, tools, training and consultancy on Governance, Risk Management and Compliance. He is also Chairman of the Board of Directors of CEME, a public-private sector skills partnership.

Alan has written extensively on issues of IT governance. Books on the subject that are currently in print include *IT Governance: Guidelines for Directors*, *IT Governance: A Practitioner's Handbook* and a series of IT governance-related pocket guides, known as the *IT Governance Triptych*.

Alan is also an international authority on ISO27001 (formerly BS7799), the international security standard, about which he wrote, with colleague Steve Watkins, the definitive compliance guide, *IT Governance: A Manager's Guide to Data Security and BS7799/ISO17799*. This work is based on his experience of leading the world's first successful implementation of BS7799 (with the fourth edition published in May 2008) and is the basis for the UK Open University's postgraduate course on information security.

Other books written by Alan include *The Case for ISO27001* and *ISO27001 – Nine Steps to Success*.[1]

---

[1] For details of these books, see: http://www.itgovernance.co.uk/catalog/2.

Alan is a frequent media commentator on information security and IT governance issues, and has contributed articles and expert comment to a wide range of trade, national and online news outlets.

Alan was previously CEO of Wide Learning, a supplier of e-learning; of Focus Central London, a training and enterprise council; and of Business Link London City Partners, a government agency focused on helping growing businesses to develop. He was a member of the Information Age Competitiveness Working Group of the UK Government's Department for Trade & Industry, and was until recently a member of the DNV Certification Services Certification Committee, which certifies compliance with international standards including ISO27001.

ACKNOWLEDGEMENTS

ISO/IEC 38500:2008, the first edition of which was published on 1 June 2008, is copyright ISO/IEC 2008. This pocket guide is not a substitute for purchasing and reading the standard itself. Copies of the standard can be ordered from national standards bodies or from http://www.itgovernance.co.uk/products/1812.

CONTENTS

INTRODUCTION

In the twenty-first century, IT governance has become a much-discussed topic among IT professionals. It is not well understood by senior managers, company directors, board members and chairmen – which is a pity, because IT governance is a key topic for exactly these people,

In *IT Governance: Guidelines for Directors*, I wrote:

> In today's corporate governance environment, where the value and importance of intellectual assets are significant, boards must be seen to extend the core governance principles – setting strategic aims, providing strategic leadership, overseeing and monitoring the performance of executive management and reporting to shareholders on their stewardship of the organisation – to the organisation's intellectual capital, information and IT. A culture of opaqueness is out of line with today's expectation of pro-activity and governance transparency. Boards that treat IT as merely a functional or operational issue simply don't 'get it'; directors who are not pro-active in understanding the strategic importance of, and operational risks in, intellectual capital, information and communications technology, are – at best – a drag on the effectiveness of their boards. As younger companies, controlled and managed by people who have grown

> up with IT and its possibilities, transform the business landscape, so those boards that fail to respond can expect their businesses to be destroyed – and whether the destruction is piece by piece or wholesale is, in the long run, irrelevant.

The emergence of ISO/IEC 38500 – the international standard for the corporate governance of information and communication technology – puts boards around the world in a position from which they can take effective action to apply core governance principles to their information and communication technology.

CHAPTER 1: WHAT IS ISO/IEC 38500?

ISO/IEC 38500 is an international standard for the corporate governance of information and communication technology.

There are, broadly speaking, two types of standards:

- a specification that describes exactly how something must be done (ISO9001 is an example of this)
- a Code of Practice is a set of guidelines that describe best practice and provide advice on how something might be done (ITIL™ is an example of this).

A specification sets out clear requirements against which an audit can be carried out and third-party certification schemes – such as the ISO/IEC 27001 certification scheme, for instance – are able to exist because an accredited certification body can carry out an audit against the requirements of the standard to establish whether or not the requirements are being met.

A Code of Practice, on the other hand, does not provide a framework against which an audit can be carried out, because it is not a specification. Organisations that use the standard can deploy any bit (or bits) of it they think appropriate, and in a way they consider appropriate.

ISO/IEC 38500 is a code of practice that has been jointly published by ISO (International Organisation for Standardisation) and IEC (International Electrotechnical Commission) who, between them, form the system for worldwide standardisation. ISO/IEC 38500 was originally prepared by Standards Australia, the Australian national member of ISO, and had the number AS 8015:2005. It was adopted by ISO and IEC under a 'fast track procedure' in 2008 and published to the international community.

ISO/IEC 38500 is a 'high level, principles based advisory standard'. It provides 'broad guidance on the role of governing body, [and] it encourages organisations to use appropriate standards to underpin their governance of IT.'[1] ISO/IEC 38500 does not, in other words, replace those standards and frameworks (such as COBIT™, ITIL, ISO 27001, etc.) that an organisation may already have deployed for the better governance of its IT; what it does do is provide a coherent framework for ensuring that the board is appropriately involved in the effective governance of IT.

ISO/IEC 38500 is divided into three chapters:

- Scope, Application and Objectives
- Framework for Good Corporate Governance of IT
- Guidance for the Corporate Governance of IT.

It also has a foreword and an introduction, in which the process by which the standard was created is outlined and the corporate governance context is described.

---

[1] Both quotations in this paragraph are from the Foreword to ISO/IEC 38500:2008.

CHAPTER 2: THE CORPORATE GOVERNANCE CONTEXT

ISO/IEC 38500 is clear that governance is distinct from management. It identifies the role of an organisation's governing body, and aligns that with the governing body's role as described in the OECD Principles of Corporate Governance, as revised in 2004, and in the Cadbury Report on Corporate Governance of 1992.

'Corporate governance could be thought of as the combined statutory and non-statutory framework within which boards of directors exercise their fiduciary duties to the organisations that appoint them.'[1]

The term 'corporate governance' first gained prominence[2] when used by Robert Tricker in *The Independent Director.* In *Corporate Governance* (1984) he described corporate governance as being 'concerned with the way corporate entities are governed, as distinct from the way businesses within those companies are managed. Corporate Governance addresses the issues faced by boards of directors, such as the interaction with top management, and relationships with the owners and others interested in the affairs of the company.'

---

[1] *Corporate Governance: A Practical Guide to the Legal Frameworks and International Codes of Practice*, Calder A, Kogan Page (2008)

[2] According to Professor Andrew Chambers, in *Tottel's Corporate Governance Handbook* (2003).

In the Cadbury, Greenbury and Turnbull Reports of the late 1990s, the UK led the way for the OECD in defining how what is known as the directors' duty of care should be exercised.

The Cadbury report's introduction provides a lucid description of the role of corporate governance:

> Corporate Governance is the system by which companies are directed and controlled. Boards of directors are responsible for the governance of their companies. The shareholders' role in governance is to appoint the directors and the auditors and to satisfy themselves that an appropriate governance structure is in place. The responsibilities of the board include setting the company's strategic aims, providing the leadership to put them into effect, supervising the management of the business and reporting to shareholders on their stewardship. The board's actions are subject to laws, regulations and the shareholders in general meeting.

The UK's revised Combined Code (2004) now explicitly states that all directors are required to 'provide entrepreneurial leadership of the company within a framework of prudent and effective controls which enable *risk to be assessed and managed*'.[3] This recognises the need for a risk management framework and leaves little room for

---

[3] Suggestions for Good Practice from the Higgs report, *UK Revised Combined Code*, (2003).

imprudent risk taking. Directors' duties in the UK have now been enshrined in statute by their explicit inclusion in the Companies Act 2006.

ISO/IEC 38500 directly addresses the governing body of an organisation, although it does recognise that, in smaller organisations, the members of the governing body may also have roles in management. In this way, the standard makes itself applicable to organisations of all sizes, regardless of purpose, design or ownership structure.

CHAPTER 3: SCOPE, APPLICATION AND OBJECTIVES

This chapter deals with the scope, application and objectives of ISO/IEC 38500. It also sets out some of the benefits of using the standard in terms of the conformance and performance of the organisation. It further provides a set of definitions, some of which are drawn from ISO Guide 73:2002 (Risk Management – Vocabulary – Guidelines for Use in Standards).

Scope

As might be expected, the scope of the standard is 'the governance of management processes (and decisions) relating to the information and communications processes used by an organisation'.[1] The standard recognises that these processes could be controlled by one of the following:

- IT specialists within the organisation
- external service providers
- business units within the organisation.

The standard is directed at providing 'guiding principles' for directors of organisations on how to ensure that the use of information technology within their organisations is effective, efficient and acceptable. It also recognises that it has a role in providing guidance to the wide range of people whose role might be to advice, assist or

[1] ISO/IEC 38500 clause 1.1

inform directors – including external specialists and IT auditors.

Application

As is usually the case with standards published by ISO/IEC, this one is written to be sector-agnostic. It is designed so that it can be applied by companies of all sizes and from all sectors: public, private and not-for-profit.

Objectives

The standard aims to 'promote effective, efficient, and acceptable use of IT' in three ways:

- assuring stakeholders (which includes consumers and shareholders as well as employees and providers/vendors) that they can have confidence in the organisation's IT governance if the standard is followed
- informing and guiding the directors in their IT governance activities
- providing a basis for objective evaluation of IT governance (and it is this clause that is particularly interesting to IT auditors).

Benefits

ISO/IEC 38500 'establishes a model for the governance of IT' and helps directors find an appropriate balance between risk and reward in their stewardship of the organisation's IT investment – exactly the requirement of today's corporate governance regime.

The standard identifies two principal benefits that organisations can derive from following its guidance.

- Conformance – directors who exercise proper IT governance are more likely to address specific IT-related risks and compliance requirements (and the standard provides a series of examples of these) in a way that enables them to demonstrate that their obligations have been met.
- Directors, though, are not simply responsible for complying with legislation; they also have to take risks and deliver a financial return for their shareholders. In the public and not-for-profit sectors, they have to manage the costs of the organisation efficiently in order to deliver against the expectations of their various stakeholders. Directors who apply the guidance of ISO/IEC 38500 are more likely to succeed at this than those who do not. Again, the standard identifies a number of ways in which IT can contribute positively to the performance of the organisation.

Definitions

ISO/IEC 38500 contains a number of definitions of terms used within the standard. Those dealing with risk are taken from ISO Guide 73:2002. The most important of these definitions provide for the corporate governance of IT, or what most people will call, simply IT governance:

> The system by which the current and future use of IT is directed and controlled, Corporate Governance of IT involves evaluating and directing the use of IT to

support the organisation and monitoring this use to achieve plans.

The definitions are all good, sensible, practical ones that will make sense to any director or manager and which, on their own, almost justify purchasing a copy of the standard!

CHAPTER 4: FRAMEWORK FOR GOOD IT GOVERNANCE

This, the second chapter of ISO/IEC 38500, contains the meat of the matter, the most important part of the standard, and the core of the standard's concept of IT governance. It identifies six principles of good IT governance, and three main tasks for which directors are responsible.

Six principles

The six principles – which are intended to guide decision making – of good IT governance are:

1. Responsibility
2. Strategy
3. Acquisition
4. Performance
5. Conformance
6. Human behaviour.

The principle of **Responsibility** recognises that those responsible for IT within organisations must have the authority to perform the actions for which they are responsible. The notion of 'accountability' is contained in this principle.

Strategy recognises that an organisation's business strategy should take into account the current and future IT capabilities; conversely, the IT strategy should reflect the requirements of the business strategy. This notion is often described as business–IT alignment, as though the requirement is a surprising one!

Acquisition is the principle that stakeholders should applaud: it argues that IT investment decision making should be clear and transparent, with an appropriate balance between cost and opportunity, with a clear understanding of risk and both a long and a short term view.

IT should be 'fit for purpose', and **Performance** is the fourth principle; IT service management is one way of expressing this principle in action.

IT underpins financial accounting and houses, supports and manipulates data on which the organisation's survival depends; the principle of **Conformance** requires the organisation to ensure that IT complies with all regulatory and contractual requirements; standards such as ISO/IEC 27001 have a key role to play here.

IT, of course, is part of an organisation that depends primarily on its humans; the sixth principle, **Human behaviour**, requires IT policies, practices and decisions to respect human behaviour (which is one of the defined terms in the standard).

The IT governance model

ISO/IEC 38500 says that directors have three main tasks in respect of IT.

- **Evaluate** – the current and future use of IT.
- **Direct** – plans and policies to ensure IT use meets business requirements.
- **Monitor** – to ensure that IT conforms to polices and performs against plans.

The standard proposes a model for IT governance, which is set out in Figure 1. This model, which was first published in AS 8015:2005, is a clear and simple one that clearly contextualises the board's role in respect of IT governance.

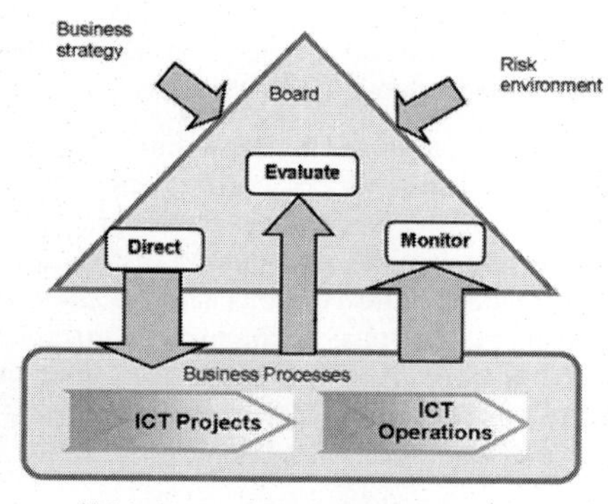

'Original image copyright ISO/IEC 2008'

Figure 1: ICT corporate governance

Evaluate

The standard says directors should evaluate the current and future use of IT (including strategies, implementation plans, supply arrangements and so on, whether this is internal, external or some combination of both). Directors should take account of pressures acting on the business, including technological change, economic and other trends, and politics; evaluations should be regular, and be informed by and consider current and future business needs and objectives.

Direct

The board must assign responsibility for implementation of IT plans and policies. The board, therefore, must hold management to account for delivery of those plans. Plans set the direction for IT investment, operation and projects, while policies are directional and should help establish sound behaviour.

This action encompasses the requirement for good, transparent and timely information from management to the board about the progress of IT operations and projects, thus putting the board in a position to ensure that IT projects move smoothly into the operational phase without more disruption than planned for. As most IT projects fail, this aspect of just this one IT governance action could have a significant effect on improving rates of IT project success.

Monitor

Those directors who want timely information that will enable them to act must first implement monitoring systems that will tell them what is going on – and which will alert them to any failures to comply with regulation, statute or contract. Internal audit is as much a part of effective monitoring as is clear management accountability and meaningful performance reporting.

Accountability

ISO/IEC 38500 makes a very clear statement at the end of this chapter: 'Accountability for the effective, efficient and acceptable use and delivery of IT by an organisation remains with the directors and cannot be delegated.'

CHAPTER 5: IMPLEMENTING THE SIX IT GOVERNANCE PRINCIPLES

The third chapter of ISO/IEC 38500 describes how the three actions intersect with the six principles; it provides, if you will, guidance on how the six principles are to be implemented, by applying the three actions in each case. Of course, none of this is intended to be exhaustive, and each organisation is encouraged to give 'due consideration' to its own nature and make an 'appropriate analysis of the risk and opportunities for the use of IT'.

Responsibility

Evaluate

- options for assigning responsibilities
- the competence of those given operational decision-making responsibilities, with a preference for these to be business managers supported by IT specialists.

Direct

- that plans are carried out according to assigned responsibilities
- that required information is received.

Monitor

- establishment of appropriate IT governance mechanisms
- acceptance of responsibilities
- actual performance of those with responsibilities.

Strategy

Evaluate

- developments in IT and business processes to ensure business alignment
- IT activities to ensure improvements and developments align with changing business priorities
- to ensure that appropriate risk assessments and risk analysis are carried out (to appropriate international standards).

Direct

- preparation of plans and policies that ensure organisational benefit from IT
- submission of proposals for innovative use of IT that enable the business to compete and perform better.

Monitor

- progress of approved IT proposals to ensure they achieve required objectives in required timeframes using the resources actually allocated
- that IT is actually achieving 'its intended benefits'.

Acquisition

Evaluate

- options for IT to realise business objectives, balancing risk, reward and value for money.

Direct

- IT assets appropriately – suitably documented, and with adequate capability to manage the acquired assets
- supply arrangements (internal and external) to meet the organisation's supply needs.

Monitor

- that IT investments produce the value that was promised
- how well their own people – and suppliers – really understand and support the organisation's IT acquisitions.

Performance

Evaluate

- management's proposed means for ensuring that IT will support business processes, with required capability and capacity, taking into account assessed risks
- risks arising from IT activities
- risks to the integrity of the information and protection of information assets and intellectual property
- options for assuring effective, timely decisions about the use of IT
- (self-reflectively) the effectiveness and performance of the IT governance framework.

Direct

- allocation of sufficient resources to ensure that IT meets its agreed objectives
- to ensure that correct, up-to-date and secure data is available to support the business.

Monitor

- the extent to which IT actually does support the business
- the extent to which prioritisation of IT resources actually matches organisational objectives
- the extent to which IT policies are properly applied and followed.

Conformance

Evaluate

- regularly the extent to which IT meets the requirements of all applicable regulation, law, contracts and so on, and conforms with applicable policies and standards
- the extent to which the organisation conforms to its own IT governance framework.

Direct

- IT management to 'establish mechanisms' and provide regular and routine reports on IT conformance with its obligations
- to ensure the creation, maintenance and observance of policies and procedures for the correct use of IT
- to ensure that staff are professionally developed and follow formal professional development guidelines (i.e. certifications)
- to ensure that all IT actions are ethical (this is about governance, after all).

Monitor

- internal reporting and IT audit so that it is timely, transparent, suitable and complete
- to ensure that all IT activities support the organisation in achieving its full range of obligations, ranging from data protection to environmental impact.

Human behaviour

Evaluate

- that directors ensure that human behaviour is allowed for (!).

Direct

- that IT activities are consistent with human behaviour, which should be obvious but is not always so
- that there is an effective IT whistle-blowing regime in place, such that risks or concerns from anywhere in the organisation can be drawn to the board's attention.

Monitor

- that appropriate attention is given to human behaviour
- that work practices are 'consistent with the appropriate use of IT'.

CHAPTER 6: ISO/IEC 38500 AND THE IT STEERING COMMITTEE

ISO/IEC 38500 is a principles-based standard. It describes what directors should do, but does not provide guidance on how they should go about implementing an IT governance framework.

The board, in effect, needs to create a mechanism through which it can exercise its IT governance responsibilities and provide the business with technology leadership. The most effective way of doing this is through the creation of a standing board IT committee. Technology or IT leadership requires a specific mechanism of this sort, in a way that, for instance, neither HR (Human Resources) nor Sales do, for two reasons.

- HR, sales, marketing, and so on, are usually already dealt with effectively as part of the existing board agenda; most board members already understand the issues around sales and marketing, and the people involved in making sales happen already get a great deal of informed attention. The organisation almost certainly already has well-developed governance frameworks for these key activities. No additional benefits would accrue to the organisation through the creation of additional leadership mechanisms for these activities.
- IT, in contrast, is not as well understood at board level and there are usually no established IT governance frameworks inside organisations. It is not well understood, but it

is critical: on average, investment in IT represents more than 50% of every organisation's annual capital investment and, typically, more than 30% of its cost base is in IT – for most businesses, the direct cost of IT operations is now second only to staffing as an expense item. There is, in other words, a gap between the importance of IT and the understanding of IT: an IT governance framework closes that gap, providing all those with a limited understanding of IT in the enterprise with a framework within which they can improve their understanding to a level appropriate for this critical contributor to their competitive position.

The board-level IT steering or strategy committee has a number of functions, some of which (depending on the size, structure and complexity of the organisation) may be dealt with through subcommittees.

This committee takes the lead, on behalf of the board, in dealing with IT governance principles (including the decision-making hierarchy), strategy and risk treatment criteria. ISO/IEC 38500 is very clear in its statement that the board cannot escape its overall responsibility for IT and, therefore, the board continues to have a key role in monitoring and oversight across the whole of IT, and particularly in respect of project governance.

This monitoring component means that the board IT committee has similarities to the audit committee and, given the extent to which IT governance issues impinge on audit issues (particularly around internal control), there is some sense in having a number of members of each committee in common.

They are not necessarily the same committees, however. Many boards expect their audit committees to carry out, on their behalf, the crucial monitoring activities of their overall governance framework. In many such organisations, the monitoring component of the IT governance framework will be included in the agenda of the audit committee, in order to ensure a clear segregation between those responsible for determining (the Direct and Evaluate actions) the ICT strategy of the organisation and approving investment, and those responsible for monitoring and overseeing the appropriateness and effectiveness of those decisions.

Composition of the IT steering committee

The composition of the IT steering committee should be straightforward. The chair should be selected on exactly the same basis, following the same rules, as the chair of the audit committee. There should be a majority of independent directors on the committee, and key executives should be invited to attend: the CEO, the CFO and the CIO (or equivalent) would be included as a minimum. In some organisations, it would be appropriate to include the CCO (Chief Compliance Officer) as well.

The other key business heads in the organisation (whether they are from production, procurement, retail, sales, marketing, and so on, depends on the sector, the organisation and the existing management structure) – the ones who would be included in any business strategy committee – should be included in the IT steering committee.

The CIO's position and level of accountability should be clear. The CIO should be on the same level, and have the same status, as the CFO and the other functional heads (e.g. sales, marketing, etc.), with direct responsibility for managing the IT operations and personal accountability for the success of organisational IT activity.

- The IT steering committee needs at least one independent director who has the right mix of business and IT experience and sufficient gravitas to lead the board's IT governance efforts.
- All the other non-executive directors should be prepared and determined to question (evaluate and monitor) every aspect of IT planning and activity.
- The executive – particularly the CIO and the IT management – should be banned from using IT jargon, and forced to express everything they have to say about IT in a format that focuses on comprehensible (to the non-IT specialist) opportunities, issues, risks or plans.
- The IT steering committee should have access to external, professional advice on this as on other matters. Employ outside experts (strategic IT consultants) as board advisers with the specific brief of confirming that what the board has been told is accurate, complete and true and, if not, what has been left out.

CHAPTER 7: PROJECT GOVERNANCE

It may seem unusual, in a pocket guide on the international IT governance standard, to have a chapter on project governance. Effective project governance, though, is one of the areas in which ISO/IEC 38500 can have the most immediately beneficial impact.

Organisations continuously upgrade their IT systems or deploy new systems to improve customer service, reduce cost, improve product or service quality, and to deliver new products, services and business models. These deployments often involve strategic risk for the organisation; they always involve operational risk.

Risk management is a board responsibility and, therefore, project governance – from inception through to deployment – must also be a board responsibility; the Evaluate action under both the Strategy and Acquisition principles of the standard is for directors to subject IT and IT proposals to appropriate risk assessment.

IT projects are not always delivered successfully. Authoritative research shows that the majority of projects fail to deliver the benefits that justified commencing the project and that, of those that do, the majority come in late and/or over budget.

Organisations whose IT projects failed usually all deployed recognisable project management methodologies; the reasons for failure were invariably to do with failures of project governance rather than simply of operational management.

Increasingly, stakeholders are concerned about project failure. In the past, investment analysts were reluctant to assess IT. Institutional shareholders are now becoming more muscular. Technology is as significant a component of the organisation's cost base as its headcount, but usually consumes substantially more capital.

Driven, in part, by the changing corporate governance climate and, in equal part, by the poor record of IT projects, stakeholders and institutional shareholders increasingly seek transparency around IT. This is even more the case in the public sector, where very substantial sums of taxpayer money is at risk in large-scale IT projects.

The Standish Group's research on IT project failure found that:

- 16.2% of software projects were completed on time and on budget
- 31% of projects were cancelled before completion
- 53% of projects would cost over 189% of their original estimates.[1]

More recent surveys indicate that nothing much has changed.

But there is more than project failure involved: it is estimated that 80% of corporate assets today are

[1] *The Chaos Report*, The Standish Group (1994).

digital.[2] As shareholders and boards focus on the extent to which information and intellectual capital are fundamental to their competitive position and long-term survival, so they recognise the fiduciary nature of their responsibility to shareholders and other stakeholders in respect of the organisation's information assets and IT.

As they recognise the impact that technology has on business performance (and, consequently, on stakeholder value), so they look increasingly for a framework that ensures that IT projects are aligned with commercial objectives and that enables companies to quantify and report in a consistent manner on IT investments.[3]

IT investment decisions (for *or* against) expose an organisation to significant risk: strategic, financial, operational and competitive. The pace of change is a significant risk. Project risks must be assessed within the organisation's strategic planning and risk management framework for the right decision, one that enhances competitive advantage and delivers measurable value, to be made. Critically, projects need continual oversight; the assumptions on which they were predicated need continual reassessment and the expected benefits need regular reappraisal.

ISO/IEC 38500 guides directors to monitor 'the progress of approved IT proposals to ensure that they are achieving objectives in required time-frames using allocated resources'. When an IT

---

[2] Testimony of Jody R. Westby, PwC Managing Director, to the House of Congress Committee on Government Reform, September 2004.

[3] HP IT Governance Roundtable, 24 October 2002.

project goes off track, directors need to be in a position to identify this early, and have the understanding and determination to call time on proceedings at the point where it is clear that the project is heading in the wrong direction.

CHAPTER 8: OTHER IT GOVERNANCE STANDARDS AND FRAMEWORKS

ISO/IEC 38500 is an overarching framework of principles and guidance for the directors of an organisation. It deals with the governance of IT, not its management.

A number of frameworks and standards have evolved over the last 20 years that do provide detailed guidance and support for specific areas of IT activity for which the board is responsible. Each of these frameworks has its own strengths and weaknesses and each is capable of being used on its own, or in conjunction with one or more of the other frameworks; all can be used within an ISO/IEC 38500 IT governance framework.

The most widely-recognised frameworks that can help with both conformance and performance include those below.

COBIT™ ('Control Objectives for Information and Related Technology') – is 'increasingly internationally accepted as good practice for control over information, IT and related risks. Its guidance enables an enterprise to implement effective governance over IT'.[1] At the time of writing this is at: release 4.1.[2] and there is a growing range of related professional qualifications.

ISO/IEC 27002:2005 – the international code of best practice for information security, and

[1] http://www.isaca.org

[2] http://www.itgovernance.co.uk/cobit.aspx

ISO/IEC 27001:2005, the international specification against which an organisation's information security management system can be certified as conforming.[3] Additionally, many organisations that process payment cards may have to comply with PCI DSS.[4] While there are few professional qualifications specifically related to ISO/IEC 27001, widely recognised information security certifications such as CISSP[5] and CISM[6] cover much of this ground.

ITIL® ('IT Infrastructure Library®') – an integrated set of best practice recommendations for IT service management. While ITILv3 was released in 2007, the earlier version is still very much in use around the world.[7] There is a well-structured and comprehensive framework of professional certifications for ITIL, which is now claimed to have something in excess of 120,000 registered practitioners worldwide.

ISO/IEC 20000 is the associated certification standard for IT service management and is heavily based on ITIL. See below[8] for more information – professional certifications are available.

Business continuity management is an essential component of IT governance, just as it is of corporate governance generally. BS25999[9] is currently the world's only formal standard for

---

[3] http://www.itgovernance.co.uk/iso27001.aspx
[4] http://www.itgovernance.co.uk/pci_dss.aspx
[5] http://www.itgovernance.co.uk/cissp.aspx
[6] http://www.itgovernance.co.uk/cism.aspx
[7] http://www.itgovernance.co.uk/itil.aspx
[8] http://www.itgovernance.co.uk/iso20000.aspx
[9] http://www.itgovernance.co.uk/BS25999.aspx

business continuity management. It provides both a specification and a code of practice that can be effectively utilised within the context of an ISO/IEC 38500 IT governance framework.

Project management expertise has two main strands. The first is the PMBoK™ (Project Management Body of Knowledge) promoted by the Project Management Institute[10]. The second is the PRINCE2™ (Projects in Controlled Environments) school.[11] This was begun by the UK Office of Government Commerce and now incorporates MSP (Managing Successful Programmes)[12] and MoR (Management of Risk),[13] which, between them, provide a solid discipline for the effective management of IT projects. Both project management schools are supported by a structured range of professional qualifications.

Enterprise IT architecture is a key part of effective IT governance and is a specialist discipline that directors may choose to consider early on. The two that are most valuable are the Zachman framework[14] and TOGAF[15] (the Open Source Architecture Framework).

There is a wide range of other specialist standards and frameworks for IT management, dealing with issues ranging from capability maturity models and quality management through to procurement and operations frameworks. See

---

[10] http://www.itgovernance.co.uk/pmbok.aspx
[11] http://www.itgovernance.co.uk/prince2.aspx
[12] http://www.itgovernance.co.uk/msp.aspx
[13] http://www.itgovernance.co.uk/M o R.aspx
[14] http://www.zifa.com/
[15] http://www.itgovernance.co.uk/togaf.aspx

below[16] for a comprehensive list of frameworks and associated information.

Conformance

Principle 5 of ISO/IEC 38500 states that directors should ensure that their use of IT meets all the requirements of applicable regulations and laws, as well as contractual obligations. The mass of regulation (data protection, anti-spam, internal control, computer misuse, etc.) relating to organisations is complex and ever-changing. While a number of the standards described above will help, it is important to identify the specific regulatory requirements of all those laws and regulations that might apply to the organisation, and to ensure that appropriate conformance actions are taken. As the regulatory environment becomes more complex, it is increasingly sensible to look for some method of cross-mapping regulations to one another. The best source of effective cross-mapping today is the Unified Compliance Framework.[17]

---

[16] http://www.itgovernance.co.uk/frameworks.aspx

[17] http://www.itgovernance.co.uk/ucf.aspx

CHAPTER 9: THE CALDER–MOIR FRAMEWORK

The Calder–Moir IT Governance Framework[1] (*see Figure 2*) is a straightforward framework that helps identify how each of the available standards can be co-ordinated within an organisation's IT governance framework.

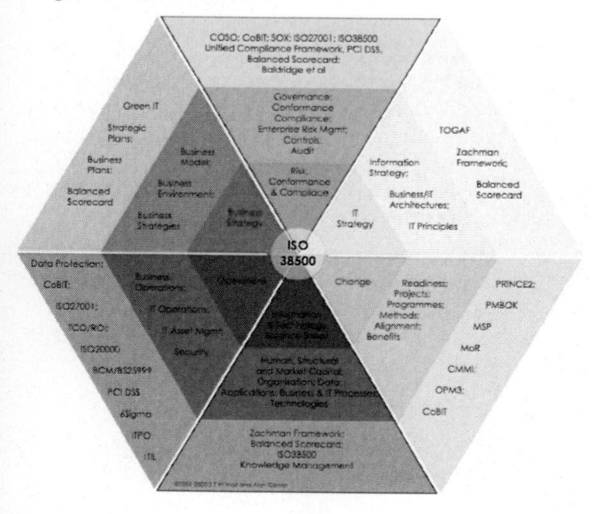

Figure 2: The Calder–Moir IT Governance Framework

---

[1] The ISO/IEC 38500 Toolkit is a comprehensive set of tools and templates that supports the development and deployment of an IT governance framework in an organisation. Copies can be purchased from www.itgovernance.co.uk/products/519.

Most of the IT-related disciplines offer solutions and tools that can help with IT governance, but most of them are very detailed, and have narrow scopes. No single tool provides a full picture of IT governance, and collectively they can provide a confusing picture that hinders the purpose of IT governance, which is to equip boards with information and levers for directing, evaluating and monitoring how well IT supports their core business.

The Calder–Moir Framework is not another solution, but a way of organising IT governance issues and tools to support the board, executives and practitioners. It places IT governance tools in the context of an end-to-end process, and provides a simple reference point for discussing the many aspects of IT direction and performance.

The framework consists of six segments, each of which represents one step in the end-to-end process that starts with business strategy and finishes with IT operational support for delivery of business value against that strategy.

Each segment is divided into three layers.

- The innermost layer represents the board, which directs, evaluates, and monitors information technology support for business.
- The middle layer represents executive management, which is responsible for managing the activities that deliver the end-to-end process.
- The outermost layer represents the IT practitioners and IT governance practitioners, who use proven tools and methodologies to

plan, design, assess, control and deliver the IT support for business.

Navigating the framework

The top half of the framework covers the processes that establish direction, specify constraints, make decisions, and plan.

The bottom half covers the processes that develop new capabilities, manage the capabilities, and use IT to deliver business products and services.

Let us start at the *9 o'clock* position (business strategy), and follow the segments clockwise through the end-to-end process.

The board decides the organisation's goals and business strategies. These are analysed and designed by the executive managers and their strategy practitioners. The strategies must operate (*see Figure 3*) within one or more corporate governance regimes (the Combined Code, Sarbanes–Oxley, Basel II, and so on).

Organisations operate within a risk environment, so it is critical to undertake a thorough risk assessment to decide which controls will be most appropriate to mitigate identified risks. The first two segments, then, describe the organisation's path and desired outcomes, the constraints within which it must operate, and the controls that will be most appropriate in those contexts.

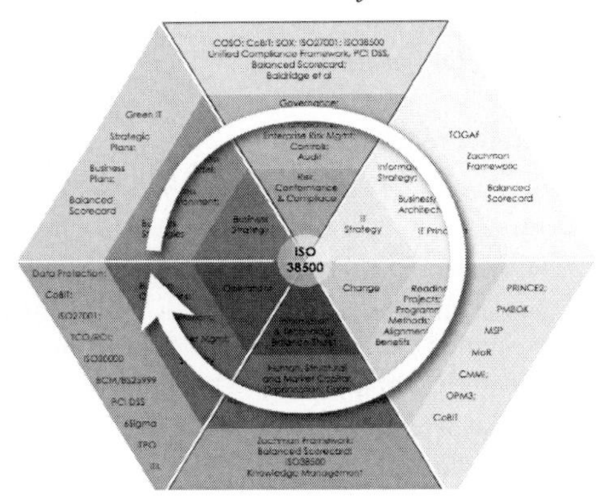

Figure 3: The end-to-end IT governance process

Once the business strategies, governance regimes, risk assessment and controls have been developed, IT works with the business to develop architectures and plans to deliver on those requirements. The result is a set of proposals and plans that describe what business and IT should look like, the expected performance, the changes required to deliver that performance, and the resource implications. IT governance processes verify that the proposals meet the business strategy and corporate governance requirements (including risk management and controls), and help the board evaluate the merits of the plans and proposals (*see Figure 4*).

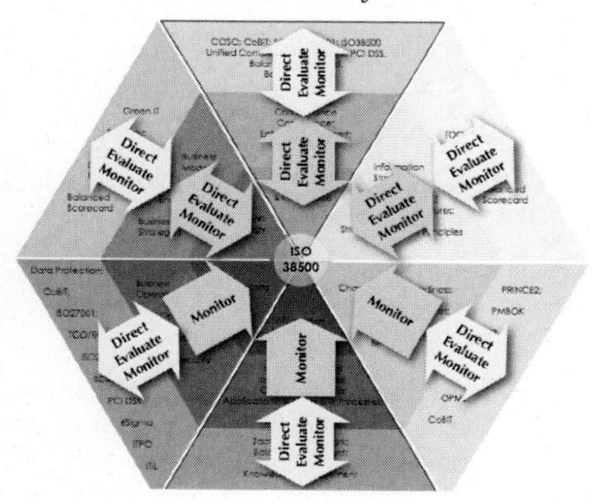

Figure 4: Evaluate, direct and monitor inside the framework[2]

After the board approves the plans and proposals, they can be implemented through a series of change projects, subject to regular monitoring within the IT governance regime including controls developed by the risk assessment process. The projects create or update the organisation's business and IT capabilities, which should then meet the performance and control criteria established during the planning phases. The capabilities are then deployed into business and IT operations for delivery of products and services –again governed by the performance and control criteria.

[2] Full-colour versions of these figures can be seen at: http://www.itgovernance.co.uk/calder_moir.aspx.

Evaluate, Direct, Monitor

As we have seen, ISO/IEC 38500 identifies three main IT governance tasks for directors:

- evaluate
- direct
- monitor.

The board evaluates the business conditions, strategies, constraints and IT proposals. It directs by guiding the way IT should be used (IT principles), the appropriate risk and compliance posture, and the investment in IT proposals. And it monitors all process in the Calder–Moir hexagon: business strategy, the business and risk environment (and constraints), IT strategy, change, capabilities and operations.

If one of these processes fails – that is, does not deliver exactly what is required – then the board intervenes (directs) through the processes in the top half of the framework, refining or reinforcing the guidelines for business and IT.

Similarly, executive managers direct, evaluate and monitor the processes carried out by practitioners, but are – for obvious reasons – more closely involved than the directors in all activities in both halves of the framework.

ITG RESOURCES

IT Governance Ltd sources, creates and delivers products and services to meet the real-world, evolving IT governance needs of today's organisations, directors, managers and practitioners. The ITG website (www.itgovernance.co.uk) is the international one-stop shop for corporate and IT governance information, advice, guidance, books, tools, training and consultancy.[1]

www.itgovernance.co.uk/it_governance.aspx is the ITG website that includes a comprehensive range of books, tools and document templates for IT governance.

www.27001.com is the IT Governance Ltd website that deals specifically with information security issues in a North American context.

Pocket Guides

For full details of the entire range of Pocket Guides listed below, simply follow the links at: www.itgovernance.co.uk/publishing.aspx.

Toolkits

ITG's unique range of toolkits includes the IT Governance Framework Toolkit, which contains all the tools and guidance that you will need in order to develop and implement an appropriate IT governance framework for your organisation. Full details can be found at: www.itgovernance.co.uk/ products/519.

---

[1] www.itgovernanceusa.com is the website that is dedicated to delivering the full range of IT Governance products to North America.

For a free paper on how to use the proprietary Calder–Moir IT Governance Framework, and for a free trial version of the toolkit, see: www.itgovernance.co.uk/calder_moir.aspx.

Best Practice Reports

ITG's new range of Best Practice Reports is now at: www.itgovernance.co.uk/best-practice-reports.aspx. These offer you essential, pertinent, expertly researched information on an increasing number of key issues.

Training and consultancy

IT Governance also offers training and consultancy services across the entire spectrum of disciplines in the information governance arena. Details of training courses can be accessed at: www.itgovernance.co.uk/training.aspx and descriptions of our consultancy services can be found at: http://www.itgovernance.co.uk/consulting.aspx.

Why not contact us to see how we could help you and your organisation?

Newsletter

IT governance is one of the hottest topics in business today, not least because it is also the fastest moving, so what better way to keep up than by subscribing to ITG's free monthly newsletter *Sentinel*? It provides monthly updates and resources across the whole spectrum of IT governance subject matter, including risk management, information security, ITIL and IT service management, project governance, compliance and much more. Subscribe for your free copy at: www.itgovernance.co.uk/newsletter.aspx.